Childhood Trauma Will Lead to Adult Drama

TRAUMA DRAMA

Healing from the past, walking into purpose

Sharonda Jeanette Jenkins-Hodgkin

I0520561

Copyright © 2025 by Sharonda Jeanette Jenkins-Hodgkin

Publisher: Rise2Write Publishing LLC

www.rise2write.com

All rights reserved. No part of this publication may be reproduced, distributed, or transmitted in any form or by any means—electronic, mechanical, photocopying, recording, or otherwise—without prior written permission from the author.

Scripture quotations (if any) are taken from the Holy Bible and used with respect and acknowledgment.

To be inclusive, you will find that throughout this book, I refer to "GOD" in a variety of ways, such as a Power Greater than yourselves, Creator, Holy Spirit. Higher Power, Universe, etc. I encourage you to utilize and exchange whatever terminology resonates and feels most authentic to you.

For information, permissions, or inquiries, please contact:

Sharonda Jeanette Jenkins-Hodgkin

Email: authorsharondajenkinshodgkin@gmail.com

DEDICATION & ACKNOWLEDGEMENTS

I dedicate this book to the ones I love. First, to God who is the author and finisher of my faith. Thank you, God, for your delivering power. Thank you for setting me free.

Next, I dedicate this book to my parents, Willie and Barbara Jenkins.

My mother, Barbara Jenkins, showed me what it is to live a life filled with love and hope. She has been my rock through many difficult events and has helped nurse me back to health when I thought I would never get well. Her example of grace and strength is beyond compare. You're the best mommy ever!

My father, Willie Jenkins Sr., who is always so proud of me, pushed me to never give up and taught me that I would be alright once the pain is gone. He reminded me every day that waking up is a sign that God has already blessed me.

If I were giving out gold stars, I would give them to my brothers, Willie Jenkins Jr. and Torrey Jenkins, who have been two of my biggest supporters. Their love and encouragement have been endless.

My children, Darrell Hodgkin, Kalah Hodgkin, and Diontae Hodgkin, who supported me through some rough times these past years as I worked through and managed to finally let go of my past trauma.

Unfortunately, since I was living with trauma and drama, their lives were tremendously impacted. I can only thank God that they could still grow up to be wonderful, loving, and compassionate children of God. Mommy loves you more than butter pecan ice cream.

My bonus daughter, Staci Mathis, whom I had the privilege of raising for a while. You turned out to be a wonderful wife and mother. Thank you, baby, for your love. It has been an honor being your momma, Sharonda.

My other supportive rocks, whom I call "my team Sharonda sisters," just to name a few, Allison Jennings, Felissia Thomas, Stacey Miller, Alisa Williams, and my other team Sharonda sisters (you guys know who you are); your love and support have been such an honor. I'm so grateful that you have seen me through my journey to wholeness. These sisters were there through my tears and fears, giving out love and hugs. Thank you, ladies!

YOU TOTALLY ROCK!

Last, but not least, I acknowledge and thank my godparents, John Jackson Sr. and Ruby Jackson, who have loved me through it all. Without their encouragement and inspiration, this book would never have been published.

My Houston mom, Macel Hilliard, who has shown me so much love and encouragement, has also taught me to have an attitude of gratitude. She is a true example of grace and kindness.

My Apostle, Dr. Dana Carson, and First Lady, Pastor Rachelle Carson, who poured the word of God into my life, gave me a desire to want to push myself higher in my Kingdom Walk, and taught me and my children how to live kingdom-minded.

Of course, I would like to thank everyone that I know because they have affected my life in one way or another.

However, I was brutally reminded by my daughter, Kalah, that I cannot name everyone that I would like to thank, so in the spirit of gratefulness, I would like to thank the rest of my Family, Friends, loved ones, and the Rock (Reflections of Christ Kingdom) church family in Houston, Texas.

You all supported me through this journey. Without your prayers, teachings, , and love, I don't think I could have made it.

I truly appreciate you guys.

CHAPTER SUMMARIES

Chapter 1 – (WHY ME? WHY, GOD?)

The Hidden Wounds:

Childhood trauma often goes unseen but leaves deep scars. This chapter explores how neglect, abuse, or emotional abandonment shape our adult beliefs, choices, and relationships. Readers will begin to recognize the invisible weight of unresolved pain.

Chapter 2 – (MY FEELINGS NEED HEALING)

When the Past Becomes the Present:

Patterns of dysfunction: people-pleasing, fear of abandonment, low self-worth, financial chaos, or codependent behaviors often stem from early trauma. This chapter helps readers connect the dots between their past experiences and their current struggles.

Chapter 3 – (DEAL WITH THE TRAUMA OR IT WILL LEAD TO THE DRAMA):

Breaking the Cycle:

Awareness is the first step toward freedom. Here, I

introduce tools from recovery, therapy, and spiritual practice that empower readers to step out of survival mode and begin rewriting their story.

Chapter 4 – (GET UP! STOP THE TRAUMA DRAMA)

Healing Through Reflection:

Practical exercises, journaling prompts, and self-inquiry guide readers to face painful truths with compassion. This chapter emphasizes courage, honesty, and gentleness in the healing process.

Rebuilding Relationships:

Healing is not just personal; it transforms how we relate to others. This chapter explores boundaries, trust, communication, and forgiveness, offering strategies to build healthier, more authentic connections.

Forgiveness and Self-Compassion:

True healing requires releasing shame and guilt. This chapter shows readers how to extend forgiveness to others while learning to forgive themselves, cultivating a new foundation of self-love.

Chapter 5 – (I WANT TO LIVE AGAIN)

Creating a New Legacy

Generational trauma can end with us. Here I teach readers how to build resilience, model healthier behaviors for their families, and create a legacy of freedom, peace, and strength.

Living Free

Recovery is a lifelong journey, not a destination. This chapter closes with encouragement, spiritual grounding, and daily practices that keep readers moving forward in freedom, joy, and purpose.

Childhood Trauma Will Lead to Adult Drama

PREFACE

This book is about my personal journey and growth through pain, trauma, and drama to freedom, joy, happiness, and peace. It's about a young girl's journey through traumatic experiences with incest, sexual abuse, emotional abuse, low self-esteem, and unforgiveness.

The purpose of this book is to show you how the traumatic or significant events from your childhood or early adulthood can stop you from growing and hinder you from moving on in life. If your abuse, trauma, or event happened in 1980, 2005, or is currently happening right now you will often find yourself stuck in the year or event of that abuse/sadness. Not able to move on until you come face to face with your traumatic event.

So, In essence, not dealing with or facing the trauma of your abuse, neglect, pain, or hurt can potentially ignite drama in every area of your life: mind, body, and soul.

It could manifest as failed marriages, addiction, and weight gain.

Fear, doubt, and insecurities may show themselves in depression, unhealed sicknesses, issues of abandonment, suicidal thoughts and attempts, mental and/or emotional problems, and PTSD (Post Traumatic Stress Disorder).

It could also reveal itself in patterns of abuse, such as emotional, verbal, and physical abuse. And when all these come together, it could lead to unhealthy coping skills such as the overuse or misuse of drugs, food, sex, alcohol, nicotine, marijuana, etc.

Negative patterns may emerge in your behaviors, such as codependency, controlling, withdrawing, and narcissism, just to name a few.

Remember, if you don't deal with your childhood trauma, you will grow up and have adulthood drama!

Foreword From a Survivor in Recovery

Some stories whisper, and then some stories roar. Stories that refuse to stay buried under the weight of shame, silence, and survival. 'Childhood Trauma Will Lead to Adult Drama' Trauma Drama is one of those stories. It is not simply a book; it is a mirror, a movement, and a ministry.

Sharonda Jeanette Jenkins Hodgkin opens her heart and her history to remind us that healing begins with honesty. She invites us to look courageously at the parts of ourselves that we've tried to forget. The broken pieces of our childhoods that continue to echo in our adult lives.

In her words, we see our own pain, but more importantly, we see the possibility of peace.

This book doesn't just tell the story of trauma; rather, it tells the story of triumph. It shows that through faith, self-awareness, and God's grace, even the deepest wounds can become the soil for new growth.

Sharonda's journey is proof that no pain is wasted when placed in divine hands. Each chapter peels back a layer of fear, guilt, and confusion, revealing a resilient spirit learning to love, forgive, and live freely again.

Reading this book feels like sitting across from a trusted friend who says, "I've been there. I understand. And you can make it through, too." It challenges readers to stop running from their past and to start running toward their healing.

Through practical reflection, spiritual grounding, and transparent storytelling, this book becomes a roadmap for recovery, showing that healing is not a one-time event but a lifelong journey of surrender and self-discovery.

Whether you are at the beginning of your healing journey or somewhere in the middle, this book will speak to your soul. It will call you to pause, to pray, and to believe again. Not just in God's power to heal, but in your own capacity to rise.

'Childhood Trauma Will Lead to Adult Drama' is a call to wholeness. It's a love letter to the wounded child within each of us. And it's a testament that what once broke you can, in time, bless you.

Childhood Trauma Will Lead to Adult Drama

-A Survivor Friend in Recovery

Childhood Trauma Will Lead to Adult Drama

Chapter 1: Why ME? Why, GOD?

There are categories of believers we have in the world today.

Those who believe that having a personal relationship with God and accepting the Lord, Jesus Christ, in their lives makes them immune to life challenges.

- Those who have lost their faith and have become very discouraged, but think that prayer would magically take away their problems.
- Those who believe that accepting Christ in their lives means accepting trials and tribulations.
- Those who believe that every bad thing happening in their life is the work of the devil.
- Those who believe that you are where you are, dealing with what you are dealing with, because of who you are, how you behave, and the choices you've made.
- Those who believe that they are dealing with issues because of some past or current trauma

and hurt inflicted on them by themselves or someone in their lives.

However, do you know that those who fall under the aforementioned categories could be right in their stance?

But I'm also here to tell you that it really doesn't matter which one of these "guesstimations" is true or not true in your life at the time. The most important question you should be asking yourself is: "What is your direction for me, God?"

Oftentimes, we tend to ask God, *"Why me, God?"* And I imagine that God is saying back to us, *"Why not you?"*

Instead of asking the *"Why me?"* question, try asking God any of these:

1. "What do you want me to do next?"
2. "What do you want me to learn from this situation?"
3. "How do I give you glory from this problem, God?"
4. "What are you saying to me during this trial? This pain? This hurt?"
5. "Who and how should I share my testimony with others along this journey, and out of this

bondage?"

Now, whether He chooses to answer them or not is completely up to God. But don't let that stop you from at least asking the questions you seek answers to. You will never learn the lessons that God wants you to learn if you stay silent. So please reach out to God and ask your questions. Hopefully, you'll get an answer. Even if it is not what you want to hear.

Always ask God what He is saying to you as you go through your challenges, trials, traumas, or dramas.

What Lord?

What is it that you want me to see from this issue?

What are the next steps you want me to take Lord?

What do I do now?

Which way do I turn?

Whom do I talk to or share this dilemma with?

Do I seek professional help?

When you're going through something overwhelming. Like grief or divorce you may want to get help.

Some people underestimate the importance of therapy. But believe me, it truly helps.

If you are going through a divorce, you could seek marriage counseling to save or end the marriage. If you are dealing with a current or past traumatic event, perhaps individual counseling can help you positively address this.

What if you need a support group to help you make better decisions? Or you're dealing with a medical diagnosis? Seeking medical care or some type of support system, as the situation needs, can help you overcome your situation.

Whatever your issue is, you must deal with it, confront it, and face it, so that those traumatic events don't keep you in bondage.

I know there is a list of horrible things that could have happened to you in your lifetime. However, the absolute worst thing that could happen to you is not being able to overcome these challenges and instead turning to some type of behavior, usually negative, for comfort.

Most people turn to drugs (illegal and legal), alcohol, food, sweets, sex, gambling, shopping, television, smoking, or marijuana.

The list can go on and on, because guess what? Anything in life that you misuse, abuse, or overuse can turn into an addiction, a habit-forming compulsion, or an action that you just can't seem to stop.

We usually turn to these negative coping skills because they give us comfort or help us to seemingly and temporarily deal with the pain, trauma, or drama we are going through.

Which leads to the title of this book, *"Childhood Trauma Leads to Adult Drama."*

Now, not only are you dealing with your childhood, teenage, or adult trauma, but you also have this negative coping skill that you have turned into an addiction.

To get help, you first need to recognize and accept the pattern or what led to this trauma.

But which help do you ask for first?

Help for the trauma, which is now drama, in your life?

Or help with the unhealthy thing you used as your coping mechanism?

(We'll discuss this in my next book, "Face your stuff so you won't stuff your face"- A journey through pain and recovery from food addiction.)

Chapter 2: Your Feelings Need Healing (feeling lost and alone)

Have you ever felt so lost and so alone that you felt like you were the only one going through your never-ending issues? What about feeling like it was too much to bear? Or feeling like you are there for everybody else, and no one is there for you? Or felt like what you were going through wasn't fair?

I know, I have.

I can remember feeling as if I was the only person who had at least ten things that were going wrong in my life at the same time. I almost felt like Job from the Bible when he lost all his children, health, and wealth in one day. Minus losing the children, I remember simultaneously going through fatness, sickness, divorce, problems at work, children being disrespectful, bankruptcy, loss of home, loss of loved ones, and a fall that injured my left leg and left me immobile, with not knowing what to do next.

In all, I had to learn to depend totally on God, my Higher Power.

I was in desperate need of God in my life. I needed Him to direct my path and heal me from the inside out from all my hurt, trauma, and pain.

In truth, I had God in my life, but I wasn't allowing Him to truly lead me. I wasn't trusting Him to heal me from the past traumatic events that happened to me. Instead, I was letting those childhood scars control my thoughts and feelings. I also had to accept that my feelings needed healing, as however I felt wasn't factual. My feelings were temporary, and they changed according to my circumstances.

I hadn't completely forgiven my abusers. I hadn't let my own self off the hook of feeling guilty for letting the abuse happen. A part of me thought it was my fault, and due to those feelings, I stayed in bondage, reliving the trauma.

Recognizing where I got it all wrong made it possible to start letting go and letting God take control.

Time after time, God said He made us more than overcomers. He also stated that He would not place more on us than we could bear. That means no matter what pain we are going through, God will always get us through it.

The Bible says in Psalm 23:4, "...*though I (you) walk through the valley of the shadow of death, I will fear no evil because God will be with us...*" He didn't say, "Yeah, though I hop over this valley, or go under it, or even around it..." He said we would go through the valley. Ever wonder why He would have us go through the valley? Well, I believe it's so we would recognize that we need God no matter what.

And if we jumped over the valley or went around it, we would be taking a shortcut and would most likely not have to deal with any obstacles. And like it or not, our obstacles teach us to trust in God and to walk by faith in God and not by sight.

Going through the valley means you must go through storms, rocky winds, unseen dangers, possible thieves or robbers, which would force us to depend on God to scale through.

I didn't realize that I was carrying around the weight of my past mentally, emotionally, and physically. As a result, I gained hundreds of pounds, both in my mind and body. I didn't know how to let it go on my own, even though I thought that I could. I couldn't even see that I had a problem with unresolved pain and trauma.

I didn't truly realize I was stuck in the past because of my abuse and current traumatic events. Or because I hadn't dealt with the many issues in my life that plagued me.

Many people believe they have issues with just the coping skill or negative habit they chose to comfort themselves with.

And yes, while they may have those problems, I'm here to tell you those problems did not manifest out of thin air. They are products of the traumatic events that happened in your lives.

The sooner you realize that your pain is caused by your past trauma or your current trauma, the sooner you begin to feel, deal, and heal from your adult drama. Also, the earlier you realize this, the better you will be as you grow older in life.

Remember, feel the pain, deal with the emotion

surrounding that pain, then come to a place where God can now heal you from that pain. Yet, this is all contingent on you believing in a Higher Power (GOD) to help you recover and heal.

It takes faith to believe that God will take your fear and replace it with faith, and that He will take your doubt and turn it into deliverance.

Just trust Him!

Childhood Trauma Will Lead to Adult Drama

Chapter 3: Deal with the Trauma or it will lead to Drama (Trauma-Drama)

My personal journey through pain and trauma began when I was about five years old. I was sexually abused by my uncle, and this abuse lasted for a few years. When I thought the abuse was over, it found me again when I turned nine. I was sexually abused by my babysitter's older son. During the next several years, I was raped and sexually abused by different cousins and uncles, leaving me feeling as though these incidents of abuse were entirely my fault. But I was a child and couldn't process what was happening in my life, let alone discuss those feelings with anyone.

I was a typical abuse victim. I never told anyone, as I was threatened by most of my abusers that if I ever told anyone that no one would believe me or that some harm might come to my parents. After this abuse finally ended, I thought I had seen the last days of ever being abused again. Yet again, when I was in college around the age of twenty, my boyfriend's best friend tried to rape me. He forced his way into my apartment and threw me down on the bed. Before I knew it, he had me pinned down and proceeded to rip my clothes off. I was so scared that all I could do and thought of doing was screaming the name of Jesus. I started praying out very loudly, "Lord, please deliver me from this abuser, help me, Lord, Jesus. Jesus, Jesus, I'm calling on you, now. Help me, Jesus! Help me, Lord."

I cried, "Oh Lord, my Lord," repeatedly, until finally, I think I must have scared the hell out of him (literally) because he looked at me, got up, and ran out of my apartment. I remember following him so I could quickly shut and lock the door. After which I sat on the floor for what seemed like hours, but it was probably only a few minutes. I cried and thanked God for saving me. Afterwards, I called my friend and college roommate to tell her about what happened. She listened and offered support while stating she was on her way to me. I got up, took a shower, and never spoke about the incident until I got ready to get married.

Weeks before I got married, I shared my episodes of abuse with my fiancée and my mother, both of whom were very loving, gentle, and supportive.

The scars of my sexual abuse carried on into my marriage. I found myself constantly pushing my husband away whenever he tried to touch me. I did it so often that it was a subconscious reaction.

One day, my husband shared with me what I was doing because I had absolutely no clue. I had no inkling of what to do next. I never sought help, counseling, or treatment. I prayed and thought that my husband and I could handle it alone. Also, I thought I was giving all that emotional baggage and unresolved trauma to God, but I didn't really know how to let go and let God take control. It took me years to realize that I needed help from a professional, and that it was the Creator Himself leading me to a therapist so I could learn positive coping strategies to help me process the years of abuse in my life.

Once I could feel and understand the emotions surrounding the abuse, I could deal with the different episodes of abuse that happened to me. I was able to let go of the trauma and the drama that occurred because of the unresolved traumatic experiences. Then Higher Power was able to completely heal me from the inside out. I was ready to be healed. I now had enough hope, forgiveness, and love that God could work on my behalf. What an amazing gift that was given to me.

I was free. The next chapter in my life is freedom. Thank you, God.

And just like me, you who are hurting from your past trauma and current drama can also be healed if only you just start believing and trusting in God for your complete and total deliverance and freedom.

Say it with me: **"No more shackles keeping me bound. I am free from hurting myself and others."**

The traumatic events from my childhood, early adulthood, and adulthood led to constant rumination, victimization, and contempalation. I was stuck in thoughts of childhood sexual abuse, emotional abuse from past relationships, the dissolving of two marriages, sickness, many financial hardships, and numerous deaths of loved ones.

If you don't deal with your past trauma, it will affect your children, your spouse, your parents, siblings, and friends.

It will also infiltrate into other areas of your life, your work performance, and any social relationships you are trying to have or build.

What we all must learn is that God is the only one who can provide us with total health and healing through our journey of wholeness and freedom.

Also, as you discover and address your pain, understand you may have to seek out professional help. You need healing from your feelings, and to accomplish this, you need a Power Greater than yourself, your village, and supportive people who are there to help and encourage you along the way. (This can consist of your family, friends, doctor, counselor, and/or church family)

One morning, I woke up early enough to see the sunrise. I watched as night turned into day, then God started speaking to me. He said, "Sharonda, this is exactly how I will remove those chains, baggage, weights, and obstacles from your mind."

"As you follow me, SUDDENLY, you will begin to see the sun rise in all the night valley areas of your life. As the easing in and rising sun of a brand-new day, you will begin to see the easing up of your healing, your miracle, your breakthroughs, the release of your strongholds, your destiny, and your divine purpose in Me. If you believe in me, you must trust me. Healing will break forth in your life, and I will cause you to be ready to speak to other hurting people.

You will then tell of your freedom and deliverance that took place, and you will spread the good news that others can be free and delivered from their hurt, pain, trauma, and drama, also. You will go and spread the good news of what I've done for you, Sharonda. You will tell it to everyone and everywhere you go."

"The hills, the mountains, the valleys, you will speak of your great healing. Your total and complete healing will continue to grow as you continue to grow in Me," says the Lord. "I'm taking you to the next level of your ministry!"

"Financially, your money will tremendously increase. Physically, your weight will begin to miraculously fall off. Medically, your body will be completely and totally healed and free from any sickness or disease. You will begin to feel like you're twenty again. Emotionally, those emotional scars and strongholds that have been keeping you bound will disappear. I will break those chains of despair and low self-esteem. You will begin to see that you are shaped in the image of ME, God... Mentally, those mental chains of addiction that you struggle with will be completely and utterly gone."

"Trust and believe what the Lord has said. If you believe in me, Trust Me!"

I believe God is speaking to those who are reading this book right now.

"You will rise from your trauma and your pain sooner than you think. Just Believe! Adonai has spoken," thus said the Lord.

For you to get complete deliverance, you must quit reliving the past hurt and pain. As long as you keep revisiting that pain, you continue to keep it alive in your spirit. And when you keep the incident alive, you keep the pain alive. And if that pain stays alive, you cannot heal from the trauma. Instead, it only grows.

This adult drama is a whirlwind in your life and causes you the inability to move on or break free. It leaves you living in regret, wondering why that trauma had to happen to you in the first place. It could leave you unsatisfied with your response to a particular event. You may have done your best to feel better, given it your all, or could have made a better decision, but it didn't succeed or turn out the way you would have hoped.

Regardless, accept it as our Higher Power's plan and move on. Learn from the experience instead of constantly whining about it. If it wasn't a blessing, then look at it as a lesson. Know and trust in God's sovereignty. He ultimately knows why He allows some situations to happen in our lives. Always trust God to see you through the valley of dark times.

With the Holy Spirit's help and the help of my support system, I learned to face my past to be healed from it. I learned to truly pray to God and give Him my hurt and pain.

"Lord, please hear my cry. I face and turn over the issues that have hurt me in my life to You. Please help me begin a new life. Heal this body and restore my mind, spirit, and soul. Help me address any past pain. And Lord, as You bless me, help me to bless others. As You have set me free, use me so that other captives can be set free, too."

Chapter 4 – GET UP!

(STOP THE TRAUMA DRAMA)

One of the main causes of adult drama, chaos, insecurities, or just plain issues is buried pain. It could be that childhood pain that we never dealt with or addressed. Buried pain that we have not dealt with comes out in many forms, and most of these forms are not healthy ones.

It could lead to detrimental addictive behaviors, such as drinking heavily, alcoholism, smoking, drugs, gambling, overeating, or food addiction.

If we addressed such trauma with healthy coping skills, like taking a nice brisk walk, talking to a friend, spending time with family, seeking therapy, or expressing these negative feelings in positive ways, there would be a lot of positive changes to our lives.

But no! We often choose to turn to negative habits or issues, which in turn results in adult drama!

There are people all over the world who are facing some type of challenge, issue, or problem in their lives that have a lot to do with unresolved issues from their childhood.

These issues, if never addressed, only lead to different adult issues that must be dealt with to progress in life. These childhood or early adulthood issues are not your fault; however, they are now your problem. So you are responsible for addressing these concerns.

Some secrets keep you sick, hurt, and keep you in bondage. In situations like this, how do you get past all that trauma? How do you make it out?

If you do not face your fears and heal, you will end up leaving one abusive relationship only to find yourself in yet another one, even more abusive. It never ends.

It leaves you wondering if God would ever deliver you from the situation. How can God deliver me? Will someone finally see me? And help me?

First, get up! Get out! Make sure you are not in any relationship that is causing you harm. Get to safety if you can. Ask for help if needed. Don't stay in any hurt and pain if you can.

If you are a child, tell an adult whom you trust. If you are an adult, get up and get out. If you experienced or are experiencing any trauma or drama in your life, you have to understand that the only way out is to face your past. Face your stuff, your trauma, your issues, and your baggage.

We must also forgive those who have hurt us, and make amends for the pain that we have caused others. This is the only lasting solution. Forgiveness breaks the cycle. You need to forgive to gain freedom.

Whenever I think about my unresolved childhood trauma, I realize that it led to me having so much drama in so many areas of my life.

Despite growing up in a very loving household, with both of my parents and two brothers, I was still affected by sexual and emotional abuse.

If you are or were feeling anything like I was, then say this prayer with me:

"Creator, the pain that I have felt over the years has caused me to stay stuck in the pain. Please help me face my past trauma and heal me from the adult drama in my life. Please lead me to any type of therapy or counseling that I may need, whether it's grief counseling, trauma-based counseling, marriage counseling, divorce counseling, or just individual counseling.

Help me work on me. I'm so grateful that You love and care for me so much, that You have shown me the way out of chaos and into freedom, in the mighty name of Jesus."

God wants us to walk in wholeness, ready to follow the path He planned for us before the beginning of time. Wow! What a wonderful plan we have laid out before us. Through pain, hurt, trauma, drama, and adversities, God still designed us to overcome and succeed. Father, thank you for your forgiveness towards me. And surely, if you can forgive me, then I can surely forgive myself and others.

To be completely free from our fear, doubt, insecurities, resentments, anger, shame, and guilt, we need to give and accept forgiveness in all areas of our lives.

What are you willing to walk away from to reach peace? Are you willing to let go of resentment and anger, or those things that are holding you back? Are you ready to ask for help?

Are you ready to forgive? Are you ready to be forgiven? Are you ready to trust in a Power Greater than Yourself? Are you ready to be free? Are you ready to let go of the pain, trauma, and drama?

If so, then give up and get up! Give up all those old patterns and behaviors of coping that no longer serves you and Get up and work on yourself. Become better, do better. Work on becoming the person that you were created to be.

Childhood Trauma Will Lead to Adult Drama

Chapter 5 – I WANT TO LIVE AGAIN

In this chapter, I want to live again, but first, I had to realize that I really wasn't living. I was just existing from day to day. I was stuck in a rut of pain that kept me in a cycle of bondage. I didn't know how to get out of it.

Here is what I knew: I knew I was a child of God. I was forgiven. That the Father, Son, and Holy Spirit were the answer. That God could and would deliver me. That God could give me a miracle. That God could give me freedom from the pain, trauma, and drama that I was in.

God says, ***"I always AM! I always was! And I always will be!"***

I had to also realize that nothing would change in me or my surroundings until it started with me; until I changed. Nothing changes if nothing changes! So, this had to be my starting point. Through this process, we call acceptance and desire to live again.

My first step was to become aware of my problem and acknowledge that I was stuck in childhood trauma and adult drama. My second step was realizing that I needed help. The third step was admitting I wanted to live again. My fourth step was becoming willing to get up and get help. My fifth step was admitting that I couldn't do it alone. My sixth step was to surrender all my pain, fears, tears, insecurities, hurt, trauma, drama, to God.

Today, declare your healing. Declare your freedom. Declare that you are released.

Jesus said, in Matthew 17: 20 " *Because you have so little faith. Truly I tell you, If you have faith as small as a mustard seed, you can say to this mountain, 'Move, from here to there; and it will move!' Nothing will be impossible for you."*

As you fight and grow out of the bondage, the struggle that you have been in for so many years, don't forget that God not only allowed you to **Go through** your struggle, He also made a way for you to **Grow through** the struggle. Key word: *Through.* The struggle is not meant to last always. Remember, this too shall pass. Yes! You will go and get through it. And yet! God said in His word that He would also make you a way of escape so you could endure.

"No temptation has overtaken you that is not common t o man. God is faithful, and he will not let you be tempted beyo nd your ability, but with the temptation, he will also provide th e way of escape, that you may be able to endure it". (1Corinth ians 10:13).

His plan is for the struggle not to kill you, or defeat you, but to propel you to the next level in your life in Him. It's meant to grow your faith in God. Knowing that it was God who brought you out of bondage, and your faith that helped you to fight. Face your traumatic experiences in the spirit of conquest; you were made more than a conqueror.

God never said that we wouldn't have to fight. The entire bible is about people fighting. Fighting each other, fighting the enemy, fighting for what was right or wrong. So, fight for your life, fight for your victory, fight for your freedom.

Questions to ask yourself:

- ◆ **Are you now willing to fight for your freedom and peace of mind?**
- ◆ **Do you want to be free?**
- ◆ **Do you want to stay stuck in trauma and drama, or do you want to be delivered?**
- ◆ **Until you can answer yes to all these questions, you will forever remain in those**

strongholds, locked up in those prisons of the mind.

Once you allow God to set you free, then all those mind chains will be broken, and you can walk in the newness of a brand-new life.

Like in the Wizard of OZ, once Dorothy killed the wicked witch, Evileen, all the people that she had in bondage and enslaved began to break free from their chains. Their weights and shackles began to dissolve and disappear!

Are you getting the picture?

Just like our demons (trauma and drama) have enslaved us. Just like the enemy trying to keep us shackled.

Now that you are free, can you see a brand-new day? Can you feel a brand-new day? Look around, let God set you free, call out to Him right now.

"God, the Father; God, the Son; God, the Holy Spirit, set me free. I want to be free."

Shake the shackles off your feet and be loosed in the mighty name of Jesus!

"I want to live again. Lord, let me LIVE AGAIN."

Now, when God made us, He made us to last, overcome, and endure. He already had the design in mind for our lives.

We have been built to outlast our circumstances, our pain, our trauma/drama, and tragedies.

There is nothing that you are going through that God cannot handle. Don't be afraid to speak to your mountains. Don't be afraid to tell your baggage to get out of the way or be gone. If not, you will find yourself dragging all your baggage around. Baggage of abuse, neglect, abandonment, hurt, and brokenness.

Remember, there is life after. Life after all that baggage. Life after all that trauma and drama has been released. Start trusting, believing, and praising God for life after the trauma and the pain.

And remember that once you decide that you want to live again, then you have to trust in your Higher Power/God/Savior to help you deal with your trauma. So you won't have to grow up with all of the unresolved issues, hurt, abuse, pain, guilt, neglect that were not dealt with earlier in life.

In other words, "**DEAL WITH THE TRAUMA, SO YOU CAN HEAL FROM THE DRAMA!**"

LET'S HEAL FROM THE TRAUMA-DRAMA!

Let this book be the starting point to your healing, recovery, peace, and freedom. For it was born out of my unhealed pain as I walked through the journey of trauma and drama to trust and deliverance. From sickness to healing. From hopelessness to hopefulness. From struggle to strength. From letting go to letting God. From many more of life's ups and downs that I journeyed through. But through this process, I became stronger in the Lord and in my faith.

I realized that only in facing and letting go of the pain would God set me free.

I learned that I no longer had to choose unhealthy coping skills to deal with my past. I no longer had to stuff my face to deal with existence. I no longer felt like giving up. I've learned that only through accepting those traumatic experiences that happened could I ever be free. I learned that allowing those mental chains to keep me bound was no way to live this beautiful life that God has blessed me with.

I pray that as people continue to read the words in this book that they also find healing, deliverance, and freedom as they totally surrender all to God. This includes those difficult things that we tend to hold on to or find difficult to let go of.

Either go through the painful process of letting go or go through the painful existence of keeping it and living a life full of misery. As Morpheus said in the movie, *The Matrix*, "Either choose the red pill for enlightenment or the blue pill to stay enclosed."

So I say, choose the red pill for freedom through the blood of Jesus, or choose the blue pill and stay in your trauma-filled existence because you refuse to let **GO OF YOUR PAIN.**

I chose to deal with my trauma by first asking God for help, then second, I developed faith to believe that God could and would heal me. I will continue to ask God to heal the **DRAMA!**

WILL YOU?

These are the insights I've learned after going through cycles of my Trauma-Drama:

- I've learned to become important to me. I started seeking help, going to therapy, and attending 12-step recovery meetings.

- I started to learn who I was and to accept the fact that I'm a human being in recovery and that I am OK! I'm Fine (Fearless, Intentional, Nurturing, Empowered).

- I've learned that my feelings count, that they're a part of who I am, that I am allowed to tell other people how I feel.

- I've learned to listen to the little girl inside who is sometimes still scared.

- I've learned how to experience the true joy of living.

- I've learned to truly love and respect myself.

- Instead of merely existing, I'm learning how to live life in a positive and uplifting way. Life is not always easy. As a matter of fact, life can be damn difficult, sometimes.

- I've learned that God loves and accepts me just the way I am.

- I've learned that my way is not always right.

- I've learned to listen more and speak less.

- I am learning how to have healthy relationships with myself and others. I no longer take hostages. No longer do I blame, shame, or manipulate! I am blessed to have healthy and loving relationships.

♦ My children are no longer possessions that I cling to. They are beautiful human beings growing and learning how to be the people that God has called them to be.

♦ I've learned that what positive things they have learned from me has taught them to walk in the plan and purpose God has for their lives.

♦ I've learned that they are God's children whom He created and gave me the privilege to raise.

♦ I've learned that I am blessed to wake up each day, so I strive to become the best version of myself.

♦ I believe my children were given to me temporarily to pour my best parts into. God blessed me with beautiful children inside and out. He gave me extra chances to love and nurture them into loving, caring adults.

♦ I've learned that no matter how old I am, I am learning and growing. I don't have to be perfect; I strive for progress, not perfection. I am allowed to make mistakes. I am no longer abused today, and I can stand up for myself. I no longer think the same; I cannot think myself into having a better life. I now behave and live in a way that has produced better thinking.

My thoughts are no longer the same; I learned to take each day one day at a time. One moment and step at a time. I follow and live by the principles of God, my Lord and Savior; I show up for myself today like never before. Determined to live this God, Blessed life healthily, wealthily, wholly, happily, joyously, and full of peace. God has turned my mess into a message and my pain into purpose.

I thank God for giving me the chance to experience this newfound peace and the "joy of living!"

I now know and will never forget that unhealed trauma equals a mountain-filled life with drama.

We will never break this cycle of drama until we first go back and look at our trauma and deal with it. We can never be free if we keep refusing to look at our unhealed hurt/pain.

We MUST or SHOULD uncover the mess, deal with the pain, and then walk in our healed, newfound life.

Lastly, remember that God's love is freely given and can heal our deepest wounds.

To sum up this book in a brief concise way, here is what to do next:

First, trust God, no matter what.

Two, work on your issues, your unresolved hurt, and pain, no matter what age you are. Whether you are a young adult, older adult, or senior adult, it is never too late to look inward to become a better person.

After which…

YOU WILL BEGIN TO WALK INTO YOUR NEXT LEVEL OF FREEDOM IN YOUR LIFE

By living in the present, finding peace in difficult situations, and surrendering to a Higher Power.

The word of God says:

"But they that wait upon the Lord shall renew their strength; they shall mount up with wings as eagles; they shall run and not be weary; and they shall walk, and not faint." Isaiah 40:31 (KJV)

Use the courage of an Eagle to help you follow your next steps and then do the work!

The eagle rises above storms, symbolizing healing after trauma. It doesn't avoid the storm; it uses the wind to lift higher. It's about allowing God to lift us beyond our wounds and find peace through recovery. Seek spiritual guidance by joining a church, talking to a spiritual mentor, or participating in a Bible study group (Do something to help yourself grow spiritually, not religiously.)

Healing means learning to soar again.

Eagles represent divine freedom: The ability to break free from bondage, fear, and past cycles. In recovery, this means no longer being trapped by childhood pain or adult drama. You're reclaiming the power to live freely, not just survive.

Freedom is not escaping the past; it's learning to fly and soar beyond it.

In many spiritual traditions, the eagle symbolizes vision and renewal: Rising from weakness to strength. Just as an eagle renews its feathers, recovery or doing something to improve yourself renews our spirit, mind, and purpose. It's the rebirth of clarity and direction after confusion and loss.

Join a Twelve-Step Recovery program; they have many for just about everything.

Having problems with money? Join Debtors Anonymous. Problems with smoking? Join Smokers Anonymous. Drink too much? Join AA.

Eat too much? Join a food addiction program. Any negative coping skill that you may have developed when trying to deal with your unresolved trauma will probably have a group that can help you navigate through healing and recovery.

Healing is rebirth; it's when broken wings learn to fly again and then soar.

Childhood Trauma Will Lead to Adult Drama

Note from the Author

SHARONDA JEANETTE JENKINS HODGKIN

As you close the final pages of this book, I want to speak directly to your heart. This message was birthed through years of pain, struggle, faith, deliverance, and ultimately — freedom. Every chapter you just read was written with prayer, tears, and courage. It is my hope that my journey has given you permission to face your own.

I am not sharing my story because it was easy. I am sharing it because it was necessary. Necessary for my healing… necessary for my growth… and necessary so that someone else might finally realize they are not alone. If my transparency has helped even one person begin their own journey toward wholeness, then every tear I cried has been worth it.

My prayer is that as you read these words, you began to feel something shift inside of you. Maybe a memory surfaced. Maybe a wound was touched. Maybe a burden was lifted. Whatever happened in your spirit, I pray you continue to walk boldly toward your healing. You do not have to stay stuck in trauma, fear, shame, or silence. Freedom is possible. Healing is available. God is still in the miracle-working business.

Please remember this:

You are not what happened to you. You are who God created you to be.

Trauma tried to write your story, but God has the final say.

Thank you for giving me the honor of walking with you through these pages. I pray that you continue your journey with courage, with faith, and with the full assurance that you are worthy of peace, love, joy, and a brand-new life. May your heart heal, your spirit rise, and your purpose shine.

From my heart to yours —

Be encouraged, be empowered, and be free.

With love,

Sharonda Jeanette Jenkins Hodgkin

About the Author

Sharonda Jeanette Jenkins-Hodgkin is a powerful voice for healing, faith, and transformation. As the author of Childhood Trauma Will Lead to Adult Drama, she shares her deep personal journey through pain, recovery, and spiritual awakening.

Her mission is to help others recognize that unresolved childhood wounds can manifest as adult struggles, but through faith, honesty, and courage, we can heal and live in freedom.

Sharonda's work blends spiritual reflection, emotional healing, and practical recovery tools to help others face their pain and find peace.

She is also developing devotionals, workbooks, and group study materials inspired by her story to guide individuals and communities toward holistic wholeness and empowerment.

She continues to inspire others with her transparency, resilience, and faith that "the only way out, is through."

Credentials of Sharonda Jenkins-Hodgkin

Bachelor's Degree, Master's Degree
Social Worker • Case Manager • Christian Counselor •Trauma Recovery Coach
Author • Business Owner • Visionary Leader • Faithful Believer in Jesus Christ

Sharonda Jenkins-Hodgkin is an accomplished Social Worker and Case Manager with extensive experience serving diverse populations in need of emotional, spiritual, and practical support. With a Bachelor of Arts and a Master of Science, she brings a strong academic foundation to her work in human services, trauma recovery, and Christian counseling.

As a **Christian Counselor and Trauma Recovery Coach,** Sharonda integrates biblical truth, therapeutic principles, and lived experience to guide individuals from places of pain toward healing, restoration, and purpose. Her compassionate, faith-centered approach empowers clients to reconnect with their identity, confront generational wounds, and walk boldly into the life God designed for them.

Sharonda is also the **author of "Childhood Trauma Will Lead to Adult Drama, Trauma-Drama: Where Healing Begins, Freedom Takes Flight."** Through her writing, she blends storytelling, spiritual insight, and psychological understanding to create transformative resources for personal healing and community empowerment.

A passionate **entrepreneur and business owner,** Sharonda leads multiple ventures rooted in service, empowerment, and legacy building—advancing affordable housing, supporting young adults in transition, and uplifting communities through faith-driven vision and leadership.

Above all else, **Sharonda is a devoted believer in her Lord and Savior, Jesus Christ.** Her faith fuels her mission, guides her decisions, and anchors her commitment to helping others heal, grow, and experience the overflow of God's love and grace.

CONTACT

Sharonda Jeanette Jenkins-Hodgkin Publications

Words that Heal. Stories that Restore.

Sharonda Jeanette Jenkins-Hodgkin

P.O. Box 14810, Saginaw, MI 48601
sharonda_jenkins1@yahoo.com

SharondaJenkins.org

Faith. Healing. Freedom.

www.ingramcontent.com/pod-product-compliance
Lightning Source LLC
Chambersburg PA
CBHW071211130626
46555CB00004B/1669